How Animals Breathe

Melissa Stewart

Table of Contents

Take a Deep Breath 2

Breathing with Lungs 4

Other Ways of Breathing 8

Slow and Fast Breathing 16

Keep Breathing 18

Glossary 20

Index . . . . Inside back cover

Take a Deep Breath

Why are these emperor penguins diving into the icy water? They are hunting for fish! Every few minutes, the penguins come up for a breath of fresh air.

Animals have to breathe. They need a gas called **oxygen** to stay alive. Air contains oxygen. Water does too. Oxygen helps animals get the energy they need to live.

Different animals have different ways of breathing.

During a deep dive, an emperor penguin can hold its breath for up to 20 minutes.

Breathing with Lungs

Some animals, like the pronghorn, have **lungs.** We have lungs, too. Animals with lungs get oxygen from the air. A pronghorn breathes through its nose and mouth. The air travels down the animal's **windpipe** and moves into its lungs.

Inside the lungs, oxygen from the air goes into the animal's blood. The blood carries oxygen to all parts of the animal's body.

The pronghorn is the fastest animal in North America. It can run more than 50 miles an hour.

As the pronghorn's body uses up oxygen, it makes another gas called **carbon dioxide.** Animals don't need carbon dioxide, so they breathe it out.

Oxygen gives the pronghorn the energy it needs to run fast.

Windpipe

Lungs

Birds use lungs to breathe too, but they have something extra. A bird has **air sacs** attached to its lungs. When a bird flies, it uses a lot of energy, so it needs a lot of oxygen. The air sacs hold more air and help the bird get the oxygen it needs.

A cardinal's air sacs help it get more oxygen than some other animals.

Some animals that have lungs spend time in the water. But they still need to get oxygen from the air. How do they do this?

A dolphin has a blowhole on the top of its head to take in air. An alligator has two openings, or nostrils, on the top of its snout.

The blowhole closes up when the dolphin is underwater. This keeps water out of the animal's lungs.

An alligator's nostrils close when the alligator is underwater.

Other Ways of Breathing

A fish looks a little like a dolphin, so you might expect it to breathe the same way. But a fish doesn't breathe air. It gets its oxygen from water. A fish doesn't have lungs. It has **gills.**

Fish, like this bass, also get rid of carbon dioxide through their gills.

Gills

A fish takes in water through its mouth. The water contains oxygen. First, the water passes through the gills. Then oxygen from the water travels into the fish's blood. Oxygen helps the fish get energy.

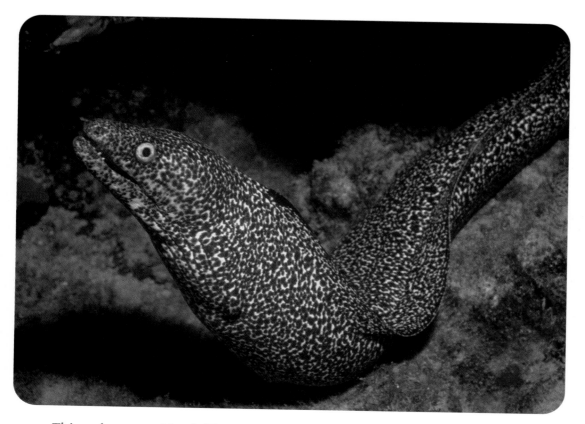

This eel may not look like a fish, but it is. It has gills like all other fish.

Many of the animals living in rivers, lakes, and oceans have gills. But you can't always see them. Lobsters and clams have gills under their shells. Even an octopus has gills. They are located inside its body.

A lobster's gills are located where its legs attach to its body.

As the octopus takes in water, it flows through the gills.

A clam's gills are protected by its shell.

Fish, lobsters, clams, and octopuses spend their whole lives living underwater and breathing through gills. But some animals start out living in water and then grow up to be land animals.

Some young salamanders live in water and look a little like fish. They have no legs. They have tails with fins. They breathe through gills.

These young salamanders are hatching from their eggs.

As the young salamanders grow, their tail fins disappear and they grow legs. They lose their gills and develop lungs. Then they're ready for life on land.

This growing salamander is a few weeks old. Notice how it has changed.

This spotted salamander is fully grown.

Some animals have lungs. Others have gills. But most insects have a different way of breathing. This grasshopper has a **network** of tubes inside its body. It takes in air through holes called **spiracles** along its sides.

Insects can have from one to ten pairs of spiracles.

Tubes

Spiracles

Spiracles can open and close. When they are open, air flows into the insect's body. The air travels through the tiny tubes to all parts of the body. The air brings the insect the oxygen it needs.

This dragonfly has muscles that make its spiracles open and close.

Slow and Fast Breathing

When an animal is asleep or just resting, it uses very little energy. It breathes slowly, because its body doesn't need much oxygen. You breathe slowly when you're asleep, too.

These grizzly bears aren't using much energy. As they sleep, they breathe very slowly.

But when an animal is on the move, it needs a lot of energy. It breathes more quickly and more deeply. Its heart beats faster, too. Oxygen in its blood rushes through the animal's body, so it gets the energy it needs.

When this sparrow is flying, it takes about 200 breaths a minute!

Keep Breathing

All kinds of animals live on Earth. Some are big, and some are small. Some animals live in the sea. Others soar through the sky.

But almost all kinds of animals, no matter what they look like or where they live, have something important in common. They must breathe to survive.

A jackrabbit has lungs.

A butterfly has a network of tubes.

An angelfish has gills.

How Does It Breathe?

You've read about some of these animals in this book. Some are new.

Lungs	Gills	Tubes
Emperor penguin	Bass	Grasshopper
Pronghorn	Eel	Dragonfly
Cardinal	Lobster	Butterfly
Dolphin	Clam	Bee
Alligator	Octopus	Ant
Salamander	Young salamander	Cricket
Grizzly bear	Angelfish	Ladybug
Sparrow	Goldfish	Mosquito
Jackrabbit	Mussel	Moth

Glossary

air sac: a body part attached to a bird's lungs that holds an extra supply of air

carbon dioxide: an invisible gas that animals make as they get energy from food

gill: a body part that fish and other sea animals use to breathe underwater

lung: a body part that animals use to breathe air and send oxygen to the heart. Many animals, including birds, bears, and turtles, have lungs.

network: a group of passageways that are connected to each other

oxygen: an invisible gas that animals need to live

spiracle: a small opening on the side of an insect where air enters

windpipe: a tube, or passageway, inside an animal's body through which air flows into and out of the lungs